Nathan Goold

History of Colonel Jonathan Mitchell's Cumberland County

Regiment of the Bagaduce Expedition

779, with biograpical sketches of the commissioned officers and pay rolls

of the companies

Nathan Goold

History of Colonel Jonathan Mitchell's Cumberland County Regiment of the Bagaduce Expedition
779, with biograpical sketches of the commissioned officers and pay rolls of the companies

ISBN/EAN: 9783337392024

Printed in Europe, USA, Canada, Australia, Japan

Cover: Foto ©Andreas Hilbeck / pixelio.de

More available books at **www.hansebooks.com**

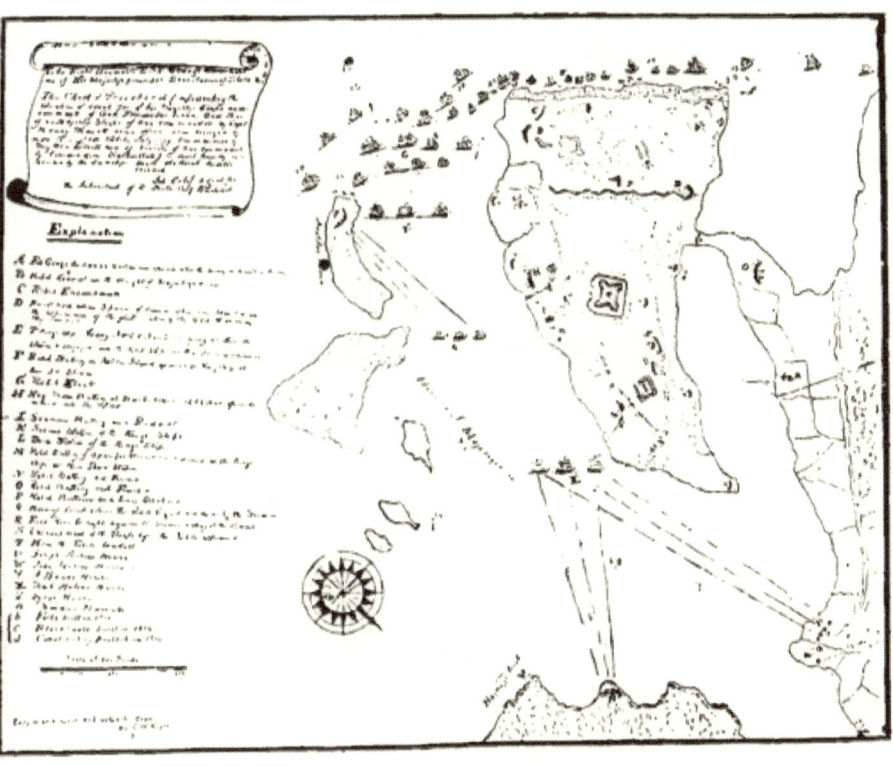

MAP OF BATTERIES.

(FROM THE BRITISH PLAN.)

From Wheeler's "Castine Past and Present."

HISTORY

OF

COLONEL JONATHAN MITCHELL'S
CUMBERLAND COUNTY REGIMENT

OF THE

BAGADUCE EXPEDITION, 1779

WITH BIOGRAPICAL SKETCHES OF THE COMMIS-
SIONED OFFICERS AND PAY-ROLLS
OF THE COMPANIES

BY NATHAN GOOLD

Author of the Histories of Col. Edmund Phinney's 31st Regiment of
Foot, 1775, and 18th Continental Regiment, 1776

REPRINTED FROM THE
MAINE HISTORICAL SOCIETY'S QUARTERLY

PORTLAND, MAINE
THE THURSTON PRINT
1899

COLONEL JONATHAN MITCHELL'S CUMBERLAND COUNTY REGIMENT.

BAGADUCE EXPEDITION, 1779.

BY NATHAN GOOLD.

Read before the Maine Historical Society, October 27, 1898.

THE expedition organized by the Americans in June, 1779, to dislodge the British who had occupied the point where is now the town of Castine, Maine, as a base of supplies and a naval station, has been known in history as the Bagaduce expedition, but at that time was called " The Expedition to the Penobscot." The arm of the sea now called Bagaduce River was in former times called Matchebiguatus, an Indian name meaning at a place where there is no safe harbor. At the time of the Revolution it was known as Maja-Bagaduce, which was contracted into Bagaduce and hence the name of the expedition.

The fact that the campaign was a disastrous failure has probably deterred historians from the preparation of a full history of the affair ; but as it was one of the most prominent events in Maine's Revolutionary history, it seems proper that the service, with the company rolls of the men who composed the regiments, should be recorded. The men were in no wise responsible for the results, and no doubt acted as well as they could under the circumstances in which they found themselves placed.

It is not the intention to give a complete history of the expedition, but it will be necessary to give some facts to show the magnitude of the undertaking which the government of Massachusetts did not then realize.

June 24, 1779, Gen. Charles Cushing, of Pownalborough, sent a letter to the Massachusetts General Court advising an immediate expedition to dislodge the British before they had time to entrench themselves. They had already given consideration to the subject, and June 25 gave the Board of War directions to engage all state or national armed vessels that could be prepared to sail in six days. They were also directed to charter or impress all private armed vessels available, with a promise to the owners of a fair compensation for all losses and damages they might sustain, and the wages of the men were to be the same as paid in the Continental service. The Board was also to procure the necessary outfit and supplies, and the following were said to have been furnished : — Nine tons of flour and bread, ten tons of salt beef, ten tons of rice, six hundred gallons of rum, six hundred gallons of molasses, five hundred stands of arms, fifty thousand rounds of musket cartridges with balls, two eighteen-pounders with two hundred rounds of ammunition, three nine-pounders with three hundred rounds of ammunition, four field-pieces, six barrels of gun powder, with a sufficient quantity of axes, spades, tents and utensils of all kinds.

The fleet when ready consisted of nineteen armed vessels and twenty-four transports, all carrying three hundred and forty-four guns. The flag-ship was the Warren, a new thirty-two gun Continental frigate. The fleet was under the command of Dudley Saltonstall of New Haven, Connecticut, whose obstinacy outweighed his ability as a commander of a fleet. On board, beside the sailors, were between three and four hundred marines, also about one hundred Massachusetts artillery-men under the command of Lieut. Col. Paul Revere of Boston.

Gen. Cushing of Lincoln County, and Gen. Samuel Thompson of Cumberland, were each ordered to detach six hundred men from the militia for two regiments, and Gen. John Frost was to detail three hundred of the York county militia to complete a sufficient number of men for the service to be performed. This would have made a total of fifteen hundred men, but in reality there were furnished less than one thousand or about the number of the enemy.[1]

The resolve provided that such men as had been previously ordered to be raised in the above named counties, as a part of the state's quota of the Continental army, should be considered part of the said detachment and in case the expedition was carried into effect, the counties were to be exempted for nine months from raising men for the Continental service.

It was a Massachusetts undertaking, and a draft was made on the state treasury for £50,000, to defray the expenses. The merchants of Newburyport and Salem supplied six of the fleet with provisions for two months.

[1] There are indications that more men joined the expedition from Lincoln County after the arrival of the fleet in the Penobscot.

The commander of the land forces was Solomon Lovell,[1] of Weymouth, a brigadier general of the Suffolk County militia. He was a man of courage, but with no experience in actual warfare. The next in command was General Peleg Wadsworth, of Duxbury, who had seen service at the seige of Boston and in Rhode Island. After the war he settled in Portland, where he was a most useful and honored citizen. He, without doubt, was the best officer of the expedition. At that time he was thirty-one years of age. He was the grandfather of the poet, Henry W. Longfellow.

The militia for the expedition was collected with considerable difficulty. The reason given was that there was a misunderstanding of the meaning of the orders among the officers. Parson Smith, of Falmouth, records under date of June 30, 1779: " People every where in this state spiritedly appearing in the present intended expedition to Penobscot, in pursuit of the British fleet and army there." Adjt. Gen. Jeremiah Hill testified at the investigation that " the troops were collected with the greatest reluctance so that I recommended martial law. Some were taken and brought by force, some were frightened and joined voluntarily, and some skulked and kept themselves concealed. So upon the whole I collected by return four hundred and thirty-three rank and file." Adjt. Gen. Hill reported to Gen. Thompson the situation in Cumberland County and in reply, he said, " If they will not go I will make the county too hot for them." Brigade Major William

---

[1] For the journal of General Solomon Lovell, with a sketch of his life, see Weymouth Hist. Soc. Coll, Vol. I, page 14-116.

Todd said that he marched to Casco Bay, July 14, with one hundred and thirty York County men, " several of which were brought with force of arms." He arrived at Falmouth the seventeenth, and found the transports waiting, and he testified at the investigation that there were "too many boys and aged" among the soldiers.

Col. Jonathan Mitchell's regiment was Cumberland County's contribution to the Penobscot Expedition. The rolls of the companies and the history of their service in that campaign are of interest to our state, especially to the people of that county where they lived and to the descendants of those who were engaged in the expedition.

Col. Mitchell entered the service July 1, when he proceeded to collect and organize the men of his regiment. Their first parade together was July 8, and July 11, Parson Deane records that he "preached to the troops." Three days after Gen. Thompson wrote the following letter, probably to the Board of War:—

FALMOUTH, July 14, 1779.

Agreeably to your orders of the 26th of June last, I have detached out of my brigade 600 men, formed them into a regiment and appointed proper officers to command, viz: Col. Jona. Mitchell, Lt. Col. Nathan Jordan, Jacob Jordan first, and Nathaniel Larrabee second major. On the 6th inst. received orders from Genl Lovell to cause said troops to repair to Falmouth to be received by Major Hill who informed me he should be there the 8th, and on the 9th they would arrive at Falmouth and the greater part have been waiting ever since, except those who living near by had leave to return home for want of provisions.

SAM THOMPSON, *Brig.*

General Samuel Thompson then lived in Brunswick, and was the brigadier-general in command of the Cumberland County militia. He was a resolute, energetic and sincere patriot of the Revolution, who for his early devotion to the cause of our independence, and his faithful public services, should be revered by the county of which he was then a citizen.

The following is the roster of the field and staff officers of the army, also that of Colonel Jonathan Mitchell's Cumberland County regiment : —

THE FIELD AND STAFF-OFFICERS OF THE LAND FORCES.

Commander-in-chief—Brigadier-General Solomon Lovell of Weymouth, Mass.

Second in Authority — Brigadier-General Peleg Wadsworth of Duxbury, Massachusetts.

Surgeon General — Eliphalet Downer.

Brigade Majors — Capt. Gowan Brown of Boston, and Capt. William Todd.

Adjutant-General — Capt. Jeremiah Hill of Biddeford, Maine.

Secretary — John Marston, Jr., of Methuen, Massachusetts.

Quarter Master General — Col. John Tyler.

Commissary of Ordinance — G. W. Speakman.

Deputy Quarter Master — Benjamin Furnass.

Dept. Com. of Ordnance — J. Robbins.

Commander of Train of Artillery — Col. Paul Revere of Boston, Massachusetts.

Commissary of Supplies — Joseph McLellan of Falmouth, Maine.

Joseph McLellan, the commissary, was a Falmouth Neck man. He was the son of Brice and Jane McLellan and was born in Falmouth, in 1732. He married in September, 1756, Mary McLellan a daughter of Hugh McLellan of Gorham, Maine, and died July 5, 1820, aged eighty-eight years. He was one of the committee to prevent the landing of the rigging for Coulson's ship, at Falmouth, March 2, 1775, committee of inspection, commissary of the Bagaduce Expedition, when he was appointed a captain of a company of carpenters. He was a lieutenant in Capt. Joseph Pride's company in Colonel Joseph Prime's regiment at Falmouth, in 1780, and commanded a company from December 6, 1780, until May 1, 1781.

Capt. McLellan was first a mariner then a merchant. He was a selectman; county treasurer twenty-seven years, 1777-1803, and was a committee to build the court-house in 1787. He was a prominent and respected citizen of Portland. His two sons, Hugh and Stephen McLellan were Revolutionary soldiers and became prominent merchants of Portland.

ROSTER OF COL. JONATHAN MITCHELL'S REGIMENT.

Field and Staff Officers—1779.

Jonathan Mitchell,	Colonel,	North Yarmouth
Nathaniel Jordan,	Lieut. Colonel,	Cape Elizabeth
Jacob Brown,	First Major,	North Yarmouth
Nathaniel Larrabee,	Second Major,	Brunswick
Rev. Thomas Lancaster,	Chaplain,	Scarborough
Dr. Nathaniel Jones,	Surgeon,	Cape Elizabeth
Benjamin Jones Porter,	Surgeon Mate,	Topsham
Gideon Meserve,	Adjutant,	Scarborough
Enoch Frost,	Sergt. Major,	Gorham
Nathaniel Hinkley,	Quarter Master,	Brunswick
Ezekiel Loring,	Q. M. Sergt.,	North Yarmouth
		Total, 11 men.

Capt. Peter Warren's Company.

Peter Warren,	Captain,	Falmouth
Daniel Mussey,	1st Lieut.,	"
Peter Babb,	2d Lieut.,	"

Total, 57 men.

Capt. Joshua Jordan's Company.

Joshua Jordan,	Captain,	Cape Elizabeth
Dominicus Mitchell,	1st Lieut.,	"
Lemuel Dyer,	2d Lieut.,	"

Total, 53 men.

Capt. Nehemiah Curtis' Company.

Nehemiah Curtis,	Captain,	Harpswell
Isaac Hall,	1st Lieut.,	"
Ebenezer Stanwood,	2d Lieut.,	Brunswick

Total, 73 men.

Capt. Nathan Merrill's Company.

Nathan Merrill,	Captain,	Gray
Edward Anderson,	1st Lieut.,	Windham
Peter Graffum,	2d Lieut.,	New Gloucester

Total, 58 men.

Capt. Benjamin Larrabee's Company.

Benjamin Larrabee,	Captain,	Scarborough
Josiah Libby,	1st Lieut.,	"
Lemuel Milliken,	2d Lieut.,	"

Total, 64 men.

Capt. William Cobb's Company.

William Cobb,	Captain,	Falmouth
Moses Merrill,	1st Lieut.,	"
Joshua Stevens,	2d Lieut.,	"

Total, 70 men.

Capt. Alexander McLellan's Company.

Alexander McLellan,	Captain,	Gorham
Ebenezer Murch	1st Lieut.,	"
Joseph Knight,	2d Lieut.,	"

Total, 67 men.

Capt. John Gray's Company.

John Gray,	Captain,	North Yarmouth
John Soule,	1st Lieut.,	"
Ozias Blanchard,	2d Lieut.,	"

Total, 66 men.

Commissioned Officers,	34
Noncommissioned Officers and Privates,	485

Total, 519 men

July 16, Col. Mitchell's men were embarking on the transports awaiting at Falmouth Neck, now Portland, and by the nineteenth were ready for departure, when Capt. Abner Lowell fired from the battery, a gun as a signal for the fleet to set sail for its destination. The transport on which Capt. Peter Warren's Falmouth company was quartered was the sloop Centurion, eighty and one-third tons, Capt. William McLellan of Falmouth Neck. She carried three men for a crew beside the captain. Among the stores sent on board for the use of the crew were seven gallons of rum. This sloop was destroyed with the others, and was appraised at twenty-nine hundred pounds for the settlement with her owners.

Col. Mitchell's regiment arrived at Townsend Harbor now Boothbay Harbor, the rendezvous of the expedition, in the evening of July 19, having sailed from Casco Bay in the morning. Gen. Lovell made his headquarters at Rev. Mr. Murray's house, where the returns of the regiments were examined by him on the twenty-first. The next day the troops were reviewed by the commander-in-chief, which must have been unsatisfactory to him as the men had had no opportunity to learn discipline, and but few had any knowledge of the manual of arms. The twenty-third there was an unfavorable wind and the expedition remained in the harbor, waiting for a favorable opportunity to sail.

July 24, the whole expedition set sail for Penobscot Bay. The fleet made an imposing appearance as it sailed out of Boothbay Harbor along the coast into the Penobscot. The men on board were in high hopes of success. The fleet came to anchor under upper Fox Island that night. Here they were joined by a party of Penobscot Indians, who reported that Gen. McLean, the British commander, had tried to tamper with them, but to their honor it can be said that they remained true to their promise made in 1775. Our commanders soon learned that the British were entrenched at Bagaduce, and had three sloops of war in command of Capt. Henry Mowat, so well remembered in the history of Portland.

The next day, July 25, found the Americans in range of the guns of the enemy, who commenced firing from the shore, whereupon our armed vessels fired several broadsides at their forts. The British, however, prevented the landing of our boats that night, but the next day, July 26, the vessels warped in, and about noon an attempt was made to land. This was also unsuccessful. About six o'clock that afternoon, while putting off from Nautilus Island where the Americans had made a landing, a boat was struck and Major Daniel Littlefield of the York detachment and two men were drowned.

July 28, about two hundred of the militia and a little over that number of marines were ordered to land

TRASK'S ROCK.

WHERE THE AMERICANS LANDED.

From Wheeler's "Castine Past and Present."

under the guns of the fleet, and the movement was begun about half an hour before sunrise, when the British in ambush opened a galling fire upon the Americans, killing several, among whom was Major Welch of the marines. Our troops replied with effect. A landing was made on the shore under the steep bluff now called "Trask's Rock," at Castine, on the western side of the point. This bluff is one hundred and fifty to two hundred feet high or more at some points. Castine Past and Present says: — "Where the marines made their ascent was quite precipitous for some thirty or forty feet and after that the ground is still rising for some distance and was covered with boulders." The marines and militia divided themselves into three parties, when a most gallant assault, without order or discipline, each man dependent on his personal courage, was made on the enemy above, against a most destructive fire, which they were in no position to return. In twenty minutes our troops were at the top occupying the British ground. The first company to reach that point was Capt. Peter Warren's Falmouth company. During this time our fleet was bombarding the enemy's forces. Gen. Lovell wrote in his journal:—

When I returned to the shore it struck me with admiration to see what a precipice we had ascended, not being able to take so scrutinous a view of it in time of battle; it is at least where we landed three hundred feet high and almost perpendicular & the men were obliged to pull themselves [up] by twigs and trees. I don't think such a landing has been made since Wolfe.

Our loss in this assault is variously stated, Gen. Lovell gives fourteen killed and twenty wounded, while

Gen. Wadsworth says it was about one hundred, which is repeated in most of our histories. The marines suffered the most. It has been truly said that this was the bright spot in the expedition and " that no more brilliant exploit than this was accomplished by our forces during the whole war." It was a trying ordeal to the undisciplined and untried militia and marines, but they exhibited the resolute courage of the American soldier. If the whole expedition had been successful, our histories would have resounded the praises of Gen. Lovell and his men.

Soon after the Americans reached the top of the bluff, they threw up entrenchments so that they might be able to hold the ground they had so heroically gained.

Immediately after this engagement a council of war of the American land and naval forces was held. The officers of the army were in favor of demanding an immediate surrender, but Commodore Saltonstall and some of his officers were opposed to it. Then the army was for storming Fort George, but because the marines had suffered so much in the assault, the commodore refused to land any more and even threatened to recall those already on shore. Then it was that it was decided to send to Boston for reenforcements, which resulted in the starting of Col. Henry Jackson's Continental regiment for their relief.

July 29, the enemy shelled the Americans who maintained their position. In the early morning of the thirty-first a party of soldiers under Gen. Wadsworth captured a redoubt with but a small loss, taking several prisoners. It was here that Major Samuel Sawyer, sometimes written Sayer, was mortally wounded. He was "a brave and worthy officer," and belonged in Wells, Maine.

August 2, Rev. John Murray, of Boothbay, then Townsend, who had been induced to join the expedition as the chaplain of Col. McCobb's regiment, volunteered to carry despatches from the general to the government at Boston. August 6, Major David Bradish, of Falmouth Neck, also started for Boston with despatches. He was on a visit to the army at the time and not connected with it. The next day, two men of Col. McCobb's regiment were punished for desertion by riding a wooden horse twenty minutes, with a musket attached to each foot.

There was more or less fighting along the line until the seventh, but no general assault was made. On that day a detachment of Americans advanced against the enemy's position to draw them out, but without success. August 9, an attempt was made by our soldiers to land on Hyannis Point, but with no success. August 13, an effort was made to bring on an engagement with the British, which was also unsuccessful. Then it was that our troops actually took the rear of Fort George, but did not get possession. The delay gave the British every advantage.

The next day came the startling news that a British fleet was at the mouth of Penobscot Bay with reenforcements. Upon the approach of the fleet, Commodore Saltonstall formed his vessels across the bay in the form of a crescent, to check their advance sufficiently to allow the land forces time to make their escape. The British commander, Sir George Collier, feeling such entire confidence in the superiority of his fleet, advanced without hesitation and poured a broadside into our vessels, whereupon they crowded on all sail in an attempt at an indiscriminate flight. The Hunter and Hampden were taken and the balance of the fleet was burned or blown up by their crews

Gen. Lovell in his journal said :—

The Transports then again weigh'd Anchor, and to our Great Mortification were soon follow'd by our fleet of Men of War persued by only four of the Enemy's Ships, the Ships of War passed the Transports many of which got a Ground & the British Ships coming up the Soldiers were obliged to take to the Shore & set fire to their Vessells. to attempt to give a description of this terrible Day is out of my Power it would be a fit Subject for some masterly hand to describe it in its true colours, to see four Ships persuing seventeen Sail of Armed Vessells nine of which were stout Ships, Transports on fire, Men of War blowing up, Provision of all kinds & every kind of Stores on Shore (at least in small Quantities) throwing about, and as much confusion as can possibly be conceived.

The destruction of the vessels engaged in this expedition was the end of Massachusett's separate naval force and reduced the national navy of the United States to the very lowest terms.

Our commodore had stubbornly refused to cooperate with the land forces at the proper time and the result was a terrible disaster to the Americans. The army, with the men of the fleet, retreated up the river with little order. Each one looked out for himself and his own safety. They fled to the woods and carried scanty provisions which lasted but a few days, when the men were obliged to subsist on whatever they could find on the way, until they reached their homes. Some fell by the wayside and perished from starvation and exposure, and many who returned home filled premature graves as the result of the hardships they were obliged to endure. Many of the men said little about their sad experience in this retreat, because it revived unpleasant memories of a service which was a great disappointment to them and for which they were in no way to blame.[1]

The following returns of the army at Bagaduce have been preserved : —

July 20, 873 men fit for duty.
" 31, 817 " " "
Aug. 4, 762 " " "
" 7, 715 " " "

Another return was made with no date which gave nine hundred and twenty-three men fit for duty, but at least two more companies had joined the army and probably more.

Williamson says of the retreat : —

Guided by Indians they proceeded in detached parties suffering every privation. For, not being aware of the journey and fatigue they had to encounter, they had taken with them provisions altogether insufficient, and some who were infirm or feeble actually perished in

[1] Standing on this battlefield a few years since, after making the ascent of the bluff where the brilliant assault was made, and while looking out over the surrounding country and bay, I was carried back in my mind to the summer of 1779 when the events that made that ground historic occurred. Not one was then living to tell the tale. An aged uncle had told me that when a little boy his grandfather had said to him that he was a soldier in that expedition. I was now at the place where my grandmother's father, Stephen Tukey, had fought to drive the British from our state of Maine. There were hundreds of grandfathers there and in justice to their patriotism and loyalty to their country, this history is written that their names may not be forgotten, but be preserved to receive the reverence of their descendants and a grateful people.

the woods. A moose, or other animal, was occasionally killed which being roasted upon coals was the most precious, if not the only morsel, many of them tasted during the latter half of their travels.

The Bagaduce expedition was such a subject of obloquy and remark that the General Court appointed a committee of investigation into the cause of its failure. Gen. Artemus Ward was the president of that committee. Col. Jonathan Mitchell of this regiment stated before them that it was not in the power of Gen. Lovell at any time, with his army, to have reduced the enemy while they were on the ground. He also said that if the British shipping had been destroyed and the land forces had been aided by men from the fleet, armed with muskets, they could have destroyed the enemy. He thought that the British fleet could have been crushed any day before they were reenforced.

In regard to the retreat Col. Mitchell said : —

About one o'clock in the morning of the 14th, I went to Gen. Lovell's marquee. He ordered me to get my regimental baggage and camp equipage to the shore and have my men ready for marching. I did so and at break of day was ordered to march, and at about sunrise embarked them on board transports and proceeded up river above the old forts. There received orders from Brig. Wadsworth through the adjt gen. to repair to a certain height, there to receive and retain as many of the army as came that way. I repaired to the spot myself but I found no men there but the matrossis and Capt. Cushing with them, from the time of our retreat to this time. I had not issued any orders to my regiment not to disperse or to repair to any particular place but only to go up river. I tarried till about sunset and no men came that way, then I went into the woods to look up my regiment. On the sixteenth about nine in the morning I set off for home, but without leave from any superior officer. The eighteenth I arrived at the Kennebec River;

on the twentieth, at night I reached home ; and on the twenty-first, went to Fort Weston (Augusta) without any men.

Adjt. Gen'l Hill said of the soldiers of the expedition: " If they belonged to the train band or alarm list they were soldiers, whether they could carry a gun, walk a mile without crutches or only *compos mentis* sufficient to keep themselves out of fire and water." The "soldiers were very poorly equipped, the chief of them had arms but many of them were out of repair and very little or no ammunition. Most of the officers, as well as the men were quite unacquainted with any military maneuvers and even the manual exercises."

The night before the assault of July 28, the soldiers had no sleep. Adjt. Hill said that " Col. Mitchell's officers were so terrified at the idea of storming that they found fault with the colonel's nominations and absolutely drew lots on the parade who should go to take command of the men and included those then on guard, and relieve them if it fell to any of their turns." He also stated that " the troops behaved with spirit as far as came to my knowledge, but without any order or regularity and it was with great difficulty that we got them into any order or form of defense after we got to the heights."

August 10, Gen. Lovell called for six hundred volunteers, to test the temper of the troops. Col. Mitchell's regiment was the only one that filled its quota, which was two hundred. Adjt. Hill said that " Col. Mitchell got his 200 with great difficulty, including boys, old men and invalids." The men got the impression that these volunteers were for a general assault on the British works, the principal of which was Fort George. The other regiments had even more difficulty. At the same time, Col. McCobb could get but one hundred and forty-six volunteers from his Lincoln County Regiment. and Major Cousins had twenty men desert from his York County battalion, and it took so many men to pursue them that he could not furnish his quota. Of a muster of six hundred ordered, only four hundred were secured, which was all the officers said they could find fit for duty. One half of these were from Mitchell's regiment.

The committee after hearing the testimony of the general and regimental officers, and the commanders of the armed vessels, pronounced as their opinion, that " the principal reason of the failure was the want of proper spirit on the part of the commodore." He was blamed for not " exerting himself at all in the time of the retreat by opposing the enemy's foremost ships in pursuit." They also stated "that Gen. Lovell throughout the expedition and retreat acted with proper courage and spirit, and had he been furnished with all the men ordered for the service or been properly supported by the commodore he would have probably reduced the enemy." Also " that the naval commanders each and every one of them behaved like brave experienced officers during the whole time." Then they said that " Brigadier Wadsworth, the second in command throughout the expedition, in the retreat and after, till ordered to return to Boston, conducted with great activity, courage, coolness and prudence."

After hearing the whole report, from which the above are but quotations, the General Court adjudged "that Commodore Saltonstall be incompetent ever after, to hold a commission in the service of the state and that Generals Lovell and Wadsworth be honorably acquitted."

Gen. Wadsworth in a letter to William D. Williamson, dated January 1, 1828, said of the Penobscot Expedition of 1779 : —

In the first place the want of a sufficient land force was a probable cause of the failure. We had less than 1000 men, where 1500 were ordered by the State authority; whose fault this was I know not; but so it was. This was just about the Number of the Enemy; but they were disciplined Troops & fortified with a simple redoubt, which was good however against a simple assault. Our Troops were entirely undisciplined, having never been paraded but once, on their passage down, being put in to a harbour by head Wind; I think at Townsend, nor had these Men ever had the chance for discipline that our western Militia had; however they were generally brave & spirited Men. Each in his own opinion willing to encounter two of the Enemy, could he have met them in the bush : and would our numbers have justified an Attack, I have no doubt but that they would have given the Enemy a brave Assault. Although our numbers were small our Fleet had an imposing appearance, I think the Enemy must have reconed upon at least 3,000 men from the appearance of our Transports.

The same Morning of our Landing a Council was called of officers, both land & naval. Some of the land officers were for summoning the fort, giving them honorable Terms, whilst others dissuaded from the Measure alledging that in case of a non complyance We should be in in a bad predicament; the Commodore and the naval Officers were generally against the Measure; as his officers were chiefly commanders of Privateers bound on a Cruize as soon as the seige was over. The Commodore also refused to lend any more of his Marines in case of Assault and was about to recall the 200 marines which he had lent on our first landing. They had suffered great Loss in the landing. This seemed to put the Question of Storming the Fort out of the Question. The next Question was, what then shall be done? & it was concluded to send off two Whale Boats to the Gov'r & Council with the intelligence of our situation and request a reinforcement while we kept our possession in the face of the Enemy & trust to the event of a reinforcement to the Enemy & of ourselves. In the meantime we reduced our out Posts & Batteries, destroyed a considerable Quantity of Guns, spiked their cannon in all their out works & gave them fair opportunity of Sallying if they chose it.

In the meantime we were employed daily, or rather Nightly in advancing upon their Fort by Zigzag intrenchments till within a fair gunshot of their Fort so that a man seldom shew his Head above their Works. Whilst thus lying upon our Arms It was urged upon Genl Lovell to erect some Place of resort up the River at the Narrows, in Case of Retreat so that the Troops might have a place of resort in case of necessity & also to have some place of Opposition to the Enemy should He push us thus far—but the Genl would hear nothing of the kind; alledging that it would dishearten our Army & shew them that we did not expect to succeed—& forgetting the good old Maxim " to keep open a good Retreat."

Had the Genl and Commodore kept upon a good understanding with each other & had they co-operated with each other they would have probably stormed and carried the Enemy's Post; & been off before there was any danger of the arrival of the Enemy's reinforcements. Here we may see the policy of securing a place of Retreat. The Fleet might have been saved, the Army kept together and marched in a body wherever wanted, instead of scattering, starving. &c.

Here we had been laying upon our Arms almost inactive 14 days when our Spy Vessels bro't the news of a Large Fleet approaching, which might be expected the next day, if the South wind should prevail. Genl. Lovell was now on board the Warren, Commodore's Frigate and sent his Orders to me to retreat with all possible dispatch, which was effected without leaving a canon or a pick axe behind, the Enemy's Fleet in full view standing up with full sail &

much superior to ours in Appearance. As soon as the Troops, the Cannon and all our implements of War, with the Hospital, were on board, the Transports stood up the River — O, then how we wished for a place of rendezvous, the Transports might have been saved. Our Fleet soon persued the Course of the transports, but soon went theirs, forcing their way through the Narrows against a strong tide with Oars & Studen sails all sett, whilst part of our Transports had run on Shore just at the foot of the Narrows. The troops landed, the flames bursting forth from the midst of them, set by their own Crews. The Emeny persuing to within Cannon Shot, but unable to persue farther against a strong tide, left those that would be persuaded to enter the Transports & rescue a small Quantity of provisions for the retreat & to collect and embody themselves for their own safety. Three or four Companies were thus kept together with which I marched the next morning for Camden, where they arrived the second day & made a stand. The rest of the Troops went up the River in the Vessels of War & Transports landing as they saw fit & then Genl Lovell under the guidance & Assistance of the Indians made his way from the head of the Tide in the Penobscot over to the Kennebec; & in about a fortnite arrived at Townsend when was the first that I had seen or heard from him since Ordering the Retreat. That part of the Fleet that got up the River ahead of the Enemy were either burnt or destroyed by their own crews making their way thro the woods for the Kennebec in a starving condition. Had Genl Lovell been furnished with the Number of Militia which was at first proposed, or had He been appointed to sole command of both Army & Navy, I think it highly probable that he would have reduced the Enemy for He was a Man of Courage & proper Spirit, a true Roman Character, who never would flinch from Danger; but He had not been accustomed to the Command of an Expedition in actual service. The Commodore did not feel himself so much engaged in the Cause. Not that he was, in my opinion, a Coward, but willful & unaccommodating, having an unyeilding will of his own.— Genl Lovell was a very personable Man, I should judge about 50, of good repute in the Militia as well as Senate, a Farmer by profession & I believe ¡ived in Weymouth. Commodore Saltonstall about the same age, of New Haven, Ct. Report said that he fought a very good battle afterward in a large Privateer which shew him to be a Man of Courage. The command of a Fleet did not set easy upon his shoulders tho he could fight a very good Battle in a single Ship.

Here it may be not improper to mention that the Action at our landing on Bagaduce might have been called brilliant, had the event of the Enterprise been fortunate. But let military Men not talk of glory who lack success. It was on the dawning of the third day after our arrival (the second was prevented by the surf occasioned by a brisk south wind). The morning was quite still but somewhat Fogy. The Vessels of War were drawn up in a Line just out of reach of Musket Shot & 400 Men (viz. 200 of Militia & 200 Marines) were in Boats along side ready to push for the Shore on Signals. The highest Clift was prefered by the commander of the Party, knowing that his men would make the best shift in rough ground. The fire of the Enemy opened upon us from the top of the Bank or Clift, just as the boats reached the Shore. We step'd out & the boats immediately sent back. There was now a stream of fire over our heads from the Fleet & a shower of Musketry in our faces from the Top of the Cliff. We soon found the Clift unsurmountable even without Opponents. The party therefore, was divided into three parts, one sent to the right, another to the left till they should find the Clift practicable & the Center keeping up their fire to amuse the Enemy. Both parties succeeded & gained the Height, but closing in upon the Enemy in the Rear rather too soon gave them opportunity to escape, which they did, leaving 30 kill'd, wounded & prisoners. The conflict was short, but sharp, for we left 100, out of 400, on the shore & bank. The marines suffer'd most, by forcing their way up a foot Path leading up the Clift. This Action lasted but 20 Minutes & would have been highly spoken of, had success finally crowned our Enterprise.

The valuable letter, from which the above is quoted, was written to Mr. Williamson while he was preparing his history of Maine, which was published in 1832. Gen. Wadsworth was then nearly eighty years of age, and the events happened over forty-eight years before.

GEN. PELEG WADSWORTH.

The letter was contributed by Dr. John S. H. Fogg and published in the Maine Historical Society Collecions, Vol. II, Series II, Fol. 153.

Gen. Peleg Wadsworth was a member of Congress fourteen years, 1792–1806, and retired at his own request. He built the first brick house in Portland, in 1785 and 1786, then of but two stories, now known as "Longfellow's Home." He removed to Hiram, Maine, in 1806, where he died in 1829, aged eighty-one years. His sons, Henry and Alexander Scammell Wadsworth, were gallant officers of the American navy.

In justice to the Penobscot Indians who served in the expedition, it should be stated that they acted with fidelity and friendship towards the Americans. Some of the tribe lost their lives. Lieut. Andrew Gilman commanded a company of forty-one Indians in the campaign.

The total cost of the expedition is said to have been £1,739,174 : 11s. 4d., and it came at a time when the finances of the colonies were at a very low ebb, and there was very little prospect of the independence of the country.

The occupation of Penobscot Bay by the British caused great uneasiness at Falmouth, and as early as June 20, 1779, Parson Smith records in his journal: "We are in a sad toss : people are moving out. Never did I feel more anxiety." August 17, came the first news of the American defeat, which was confirmed the next day.

Col. Enoch Freeman sent the following letter to the Council at Boston, August 18. For the first five years of the Revolutionary war Massachusetts was governed by a committee of the Council.

FALMOUTH, Aug. 18, 1779.

SIR :—The invasion of the Penobscot under a very considerable force of the enemy, their progress there and the ravages committed by them in other places at the Eastern part of this State make us apprehensive that they have a design to cut it off from the other part of the State and either annex it to the Province of Nova Scotia, or form it into a separate government under the British Administration.

Under such apprehensions, a number of gentlemen from most of the towns in this County, this day assembled in Convention in this town, to consult what is proper to be done for our safety and defence.

We think that the Harbor here would be of such importance to the enemy, in the execution of what we judge to be their grand design, that they will not much longer neglect to attempt to possess themselves of it, and make it a place of Rendezvous for their troops and ships of Force.—And we are sorry to inform your Honors that such is the state of our fortifications and such the weakness of our Force, that unless some measures are immediately entered into for our protection and defence, we fear we shall fall a prey to their rage and malice. We therefore humbly pray that your Honors would take our case into your serious consideration and order that such steps may be taken as will put us in a good position of defence.

We have recommended to the several towns in this County to raise immediately their respective proportions of one hundred men, to repair the forts here and build others in such places as a Committee (whom we have appointed for the purpose) shall best judge, and we trust the General Court will make provisions for paying them for their services.

And we would request that the Honorable Council would appoint and send as soon as possible, some experienced faithful engineer to take the oversight of the work.

We would further pray that at least two hundred men might be ordered here from the County of York or some other County to the southward of us, to increase our strength. which is already much reduced.

We also think it necessary that a number of cannon and a suitable quantity of military storesmaould be procured and sent here to be placed in such Forts as may be erected, and also field pieces, (two we think necessary) And as provisions are extremely scarce here and it would be almost impossible to collect on an emergency as much as might be wanted, we think it absolutely necessary that a Magazine thereof should be provided and placed in a proper part of the town, to be used when an alarm should require it.

I am, in the name and behalf of the Committee, Your Honor's most obedient and humble serv't

ENOCH FREEMAN.

We have this minute received advice (by the bearer who hands you this and who will communicate to you personally) of the unhappy loss of our fleet at Penobscot.

To the above the Council sent the following reply :—

COUNCIL CHAMBER (BOSTON), 26th Aug. 1779.

SIR :—Your letter of the 18th inst was received and the Council have so far complied with your request as to order Col. Jackson's regiment to be stationed at Falmouth for the present and have ordered the necessary stores to be forwarded for their use without loss of time.

J. POWELL *President.*

Col. Freeman.

Hon. Jeremiah Powell[1] lived at North Yarmouth, Maine. He was born June 3, 1720, married Sarah Bromfield, September 15, 1768, and died September 17, 1784, aged sixty-four years. They were buried in the Powell tomb, now unmarked, in the cemetery "under the ledge," at what is now Yarmouth. This tomb is back of Deacon Jacob Mitchell's tomb.

[1] For the Powell family and their history, see Maine Historical Society Collection, First Series, Vol. VII, Page 233 and Old Times in North Yarmouth, Page 1163.

Col. Powell was lieutenant colonel in Col. Samuel Waldo, Jr.'s, regiment in 1762, eleven years in the General Court, twelve years in the Provincial Council, first president of the Massachusetts senate under the Constitution, and nineteen years judge of the Court of Common Pleas, from 1763 to 1781. He was a zealous patriot of the Revolution and lived only to see his country start on the basis of liberty. His grave should be marked by some memorial calling attention to him, his virtues, and his distinguished services to his country.

The Rev. John Murray, the chaplain,[1] wrote from Brunswick to Jeremiah Powell, Esq., under date of August 21, 1779 :—

Our case is very bad. Hundred of families are now starving in the woods, their all left behind them, all will despair and the majority will quit the country and the rest will revolt if something vigorous be not done to protect them from the insolence of the triumping foe who are carrying fire and desolation wherever they come. A large reinforcement of men, intrenching tools, cannon, ammunition and provisions is absolutely necessary to save us. Not a moment is to be lost. A very little delay will put us beyond remedy, but if we are immediately relieved this little disaster need not discourage us. It will, if we act with proper spirit, issue in our good.

In the latter part of August, Col. Mitchell's regiment had reached Falmouth Neck, but arrived there in a disorganized and demoralized condition. Three companies were retained for a garrison and twenty men of Capt. Curtis company were stationed at Harpswell. All others were discharged.

[1]The original letter is in the Massachusetts Archives, Vol. CXLV, Page 140.

Col. Henry Jackson's Continental regiment, which had been ordered from Rhode Island to reenforce the expedition, learned of the disaster off Kittery while on their way. They went into camp at that place. It was then thought that the British, elated at their success, would proceed to Casco Bay and attempt the capture of Falmouth Neck. This of course caused much alarm at that settlement. Col. Jackson's regiment was ordered to march to Falmouth, from Kittery, and arrived there the twenty-seventh, and went into camp on Munjoy Hill, above the Eastern Cemetery, much to the relief of the inhabitants. This regiment had four hundred well uniformed and equipped men and had then participated in the battles of Monmouth and Quaker Hill. This was probably the only fully uniformed and equipped regiment the people of Falmouth saw during the war.

Col. Jackson wrote the next day after his arrival : —

I find this town and harbor is by no means in a state of defence as but a few of the cannons are fit for any long service. To make this post defencible it will be necessary to have a number of heavy cannon immediately sent here : the militia are exceedingly destitute of arms, ammunition and accoutrements as I find by enquiry that not more than one-half are armed or accoutred.

The committee of safety of Falmouth addressed the following letter to the Council : —

Falmouth, 30 August, 1779.

Sir: The Committee of Safety &c for Falmouth would inform the Honorable Board of their embarresments and beg their direction. The return of the seamen from Penobscot in the greatest distress imaginable has obliged us to act as commissary, quartermaster, &c, &c. To furnish them with necessary provisions and to relieve their distresses we have been obliged to issue some impress warrants: some provisions we have purchased and some we have borrowed. We have observed the strictest economy and order that necessary confusion would admit of; the men returned without officers, without orders.

We shall transmit an account of our doings as soon as the men have been done returning.

Col. Jackson applies to us for some assistance where he has not proper officers to supply them. This however gives us but little trouble : but the militia who have returned from Penobscot are ordered to this place : they are not properly attended with their officers and those who do attend them have not proper directions what to do with their men : they apply to the Committee. The Committee know of no business they have with them ; here we are much embarrassed. We have also frequent applications from expresses for assistance, or sometimes are obliged to send off expresses ourselves New appplications of various kinds are daily made to us and new difficulties arise. In short, affairs here are in the wildest confusion. We wish for the direction and assistance of the Hon. Board.

We are &c

The Committee of Safety &c for Falmouth,

Stephen Hall, Chairman.

Hon. Jer. Powell,
    Pres. of Council.

Col. Jackson's regiment started on their march to Boston, September 7, as all danger of an attack seemed to be over; but a portion of Col. Mitchell's still remained.

The selectmen and the committee of the town sent the following letter to the Council :—

FALMOUTH, SEPT. 13, 1779.

To the Honorable Council of
    State of Massachusetts Bay.

The Selectmen and Committee of Safety at Falmouth beg leave to inform the Honorable Board of the receipt of their letter of the

3rd inst. The enclosed directed to Brig'r Thompson was immediately forwarded. It is now seven days since, but we have not heard of his taking any measures towards raising the three hundred men to be stationed at Falmouth.

The letter from the Hon. Council to Col. Jackson in his absence we took the liberty to open: in answer to which we would inform your Honors that the Regt. from Penobscot was ordered by Gen'l Lovell to Falmouth to guard from this place to Harpswell and to be under the direction of the Committee of Safety at Falmouth.

As a greater part of these were destitute of arms and accoutrements, the Committee thought proper to discharge five of the companies except 20 of the company commanded by Capt. Curtis of Harpswell, who are kept guard at that post. The remaining three companies which were best armed and accouted are now stationed at this place and at Cape Elizabeth.

We esteem it a duty incumbrent on us to inform your Honors that the militia in this County are at present in a situation incapable of defending us in the case of an attack, principally owing to their ignorance and neglect of some of the principal officers of the Brigade.

A convention of this County is to be held next Friday when proper representation of the state of the militia will be made to the Hon'ble Court. We are with sentiments of respect

        Your Honors most obed't serv't,

By order in behalf of the Selectmen,

                Benjamin Titcomb.

And Committee of Safety

                Stephen Hall Chairman.

P. S. A number of small arms and cartridges has lately been received, also a quantity of ordinance goods, adressed to Col. Jackson by the Board of War a particular return of which shall be made by the first opportunity.

In Council, Sept. 22, 1779. Read and sent down.

                John Avery D. Secr'y.

WILLIAM MOODY of Falmouth, kept a journal during his service in Col. Mitchell's regiment, recording each day the events that came under his observation. It is worthy of preservation. Mr. Moody was the drummer of Capt. Peter Warren's company. He had served in Col. Edmund Phinney's 31st regiment of foot at Cambridge in 1775, in Capt. Abner Lowell's Matross company at Falmouth Neck in 1776, 1777 and 1778, and in Capt. Joseph Pride's company in Col. Joseph Prime's regiment at the same place in 1780. He was in the service in the early part of 1781, and went on a cruise in the privateer Fox, in April of that year.

Mr. Moody was the son of Enoch and Ann (Weeks) Moody of Falmouth, and was born February 16, 1756. He married Mary Young, in 1783, and had children, Enoch, William and Nancy. He married for his second wife, Rachel Riggs in 1804, and had a son, Edward. He died February 16, 1821, aged sixty-five years. His father, Enoch Moody, was the chairman of the committee at Falmouth in the Revolution, and his four brothers, Enoch, Jr., Benjamin, Nathaniel and Lemuel, were Revolutionary soldiers.

William Moody was a thoughtful and observing man to whom we should feel grateful for chronicling his experiences for our instruction.

WILLIAM MOODY'S JOURNAL.

1779.

July 2. A detachment of 40 men to go to Major Bag a Duce.

3. Turned out as a Volunteer to go to Penobscot with Capt. Peter Warren.

9. Turned out in the morning for Exercise.

10. Our Regt. paraded and arranged Capt. Warren's the first company.

14. The transports with 2 brigs & a sloop, a prize with 10 guns, arrived here to carry the Troops. Drew one day's allowance.

15. Drew 4 days' allowance.

16. Our Company embarked on board the sloop [Centurion] and hauled off, Capt. [William] McLellan master. [He was a son of Brice McLellan of Falmouth Neck.]

17. On shore to draw allowance and took it. Stayed all night.

19. I went on board of the Sloop Centurion [80½ tons] at sunrise. Embarked for Majibigwaduce. Weighed anchor at 8 oclock. Capt. [Abner] Lowell fired an 18 pounder for all hands on board. Arrived at Townsend [Boothbay] at 6 oclock.

20. Last night a soldier fired a gun and blowed his hand off, died. The Hampden a 20 gun ship arrived.

21. Went ashore to prayers. Parson [Thomas] Lancaster prayed and we sang. Between 30 & 40 sail of armed ships & Transports at Townsend.

22. Regt. paraded ashore and Gen. [Solomon] Lovell reviewed them.

24. Admiral [Dudley Saltonstall] fired a gun about 4 oclock, the whole fleet under sail. Came to anchor at 9 o'clock at night under the Upper Fox Island.

25. Made sail for Bagaduce at 8 oclock. Came to anchor in Penobscot. The enemy fired from the shore with muskets. The ships ran in by the Forts and fired many broadsides. Seven of our boats that went to land got almost ashore. The enemy lay in ambush and fired upon us and killed an indian.

26. Our vessels warped in. We embarked our boats at 12 oclock. Kept off and on till sunset. [It is stated that the time was about 6 o'clock.] Come under the Admiral's [Frigate Warren] stern, then put off for an island [Nautilus] within point blank shot of the enemy's fort. As our boats were going across, the enemy sunk one boat by a (chain) shot and Major Daniel Littlefield [of Wells] and two others were drowned.

28. At day-break had orders to land under cover of our guns on board the shipping. Commenced landing half an hour before sunrise. The enemy lay in ambush and firing upon us killed 1 capt. [probably Major Welch] of marines belonging to the Admiral and several others. We took 3 prisoners and killed 7. Have possession

of the ground and soon hope to have all their works.[1] 2 men wounded, one lost his leg and the other his arm. Went over to the Island after [Samuel] Knight. He was sick there.

29. The enemy throw shells. Loss and wounded in the attack [of 28th] about 30. Lost 1 man this afternoon.

30. Hauled up on the hill [over the high bluff where they landed] 2 eighteen pounders. A deserter came in from the enemy last night; he says the British force does not exceed 350. [This was not one half of the number of their men.]

31. Two seamen wounded with a shell who belongs to the Active. One of the marines belonging to the [frigate] Warren deserted to the enemy. Last night went out with a detachment of 88 men. Marched on to the parade at sunset and kept under arms till 2 o'clock [A. M.]. We then attacked one of the enemy's redoubts which we carried with the loss of a few men. We killed several of the enemy and took 18 prisoners. Capt. [Nathan] Merrill of our Regt. took one prisoner, a corporal of the enemy.

Sunday, Aug. 1. Major [Samuel] Sawyer of the York [county] forces mortally wounded. He died this day.

2. Mr. Wheeler Riggs [of Falmouth Neck] was killed this afternoon. One of the train badly wounded. Buried Mr. Riggs very decently. [He was stooping over fixing a gun carriage when a cannon ball hit a tree near, glanced and struck him on the back of his neck. He was the only Falmouth soldier killed in the expedition.]

3. Gen. Lovell sent a flag to the lines to enquire after a Lieut. of Marines belonging to the Vengence who was missing after the battle of Sunday last [Aug. 1]. The answer returned was that the Lieut. was wounded in battle and died yesterday.

Wed. 4. Three of Capt. [Nehemiah] Curtis' men deserted. William Harper had a musket ball shot through his coat by the enemy while on picket guard.

[1] The above was the gallant assault made by the four hundred marines and militia over the precipitous bank at "Trask's Rock," and which was over in twenty minutes. The large granite boulder on the shore, now called "Trask's Rock," was named for a fifer-boy named Israel Trask, who took shelter behind it, playing his fife while his comrades made the ascent. It was said that he did not lose a note of the tune he was playing during the whole time. Capt. John Hinkley of Georgetown, of Col. McCobb's regiment, was killed while standing on this rock urging on the men.

5. An indian killed by the enemy, one taken prisoner. Capt. [David] Bradish from Falmouth to see us.

6. Capt. Bradish and his crew left us. [He was sent to Boston.]

7. Smart cannonading. Marched down towards the fort of the enemy about three o'clock. A party of about 100 sallied out. Gen. Lovell ordered a retreat to draw them out, but they immediately ran back to their entrenchment. One man belonging to Col. [Samuel] McCobb's Regt. wounded.

Monday, 9. Attempted to land on Hyannis Point, opposite the enemy, but were prevented by the annoyance of the enemy in ambush.

11. Last night [10th] 20 of Major (Nathaniel) Cousins' Regt. deserted. One of the enemy deserted.

12. Major Cousins' men brought back last night.

13. Made another demonstration upon the lines of the enemy, but could not bring on an engagement. Capt. Woodman slightly wounded. [It is not known who he was. Perhaps the writer made a error in the name.]

14. News that the fleet of the enemy are at the mouth of the the [Penobscot] Bay. We began our retreat about one o'clock. Ran with our Ships and Transports to Fort Penobscot and called on the Commissary for provisions. The enemy in sight and under cloud of sail. Some of our Ships are taken and some are run ashore. I took the boats and went on board the Centurion for provisions and then put ashore, landed it and then took off the men. Our people set fire to the shipping and then took to the woods. Our company [Capt. Peter Warren's] encamped in the woods. Took what provisions we could carry. Had 4 prisoners to guard.

Sunday, 15. Took up our line of march at daybreak, lost our way and came across about 200 of our Regt. and sailors and marines. Went across a large meadow ; struck a road in the woods and kept on till 7 o'clock ; took breakfast and proceeded on to Belfast where we arrived at 12 o'clock. Exceedingly warm. Came to a river and crossed in canoes. Capt. Warren purchased 2 sheep and paid 18 dollars for them. Took dinner. Arrived at a fine plantation and had a good dish of tea. Gen. [Peleg]

Wadsworth and Capt. [Ebenezer] Buck supped with us. Had a fine barn to sleep in and rested comfortably.

16. Marched early through marshes, beaches and thick woods, over mountains and valleys to Ducktrap [Northport] where we arrived, the sun an hour high. P. M. One of our prisoners deserted this morning.

17. Set off early and traveled by the shore. Halted by Gen. Wadsworth's orders. Arrived at the westerly part of Camden at 1 o'clock. The place called Clam Cove. [Went to] Headquarters and drew an allowance of fresh beef. Turned out a Sergeant's Guard and took possession of a large barn for our barracks.

18. Heard that Gen. Lovell and Admiral Saltonstall were taken by the enemy. [A rumor only.] Capt. [William] Cobb and his company arrived here at 12 o'clock. [Daniel] Mussey started for Falmouth.

19. Mr. [Somers] Shattuck and Stephen Tukey arrived this morning, says Woodbury Storer was taken on board the Hampden. Mr. Shattuck and Houchin Tukey started for home. Order for Capt. Warren to march to West Shore South West Gigg. [Stephen Tukey was the son of John and Abigail (Sweetser) Tukey of Falmouth Neck, and was born July 6, 1754, married, in 1780, Hannah Cushing, and died July 8, 1826. He was the writer's great grandfather. Houchin Tukey was his brother.]

20. Marched to Col. [Mason] Wheaton's, 6 miles. Set a corporal's guard. Here is a double saw mill and grist mill.

Sunday. 22. Lieut. [Peter] Babb set off for home or Falmouth with some four men because we had no provisions. [Zach.] Baker, [John] Clough, Thomas Harper, [Benjamin] Mussey and myself [William Moody] started for St. George between 11 and 12 o'clock.

24. Arrived at New Meadows and put up at one Capt. Curtis' where we were hospitably entertained.

26. Capt. Warren arrived home, [and probably the whole company].

Among the curious facts concerning the Bagaduce Expedition worthy of attention, are the bills of

FORT GEORGE.

From Wheeler's "Castine Past and Present," Showing Its Condition To-day.

Thaddeus Broad and Joanna Frost, two famous Falmouth tavern keepers of the time, " for victualling " the retreating soldiers and sailors. Broad's account amounted to eighty-nine pounds, fourteen shillings, and Mrs. Frost's was for one hundred and eighty-six meals at twelve shillings each, amounting to one hundred eleven pounds, twelve shillings.

Sir John Moore, who was killed at Corunna, Spain, in 1806, made famous by his funeral ode, was a lieutenant in the Eighty-second regiment of the British Army, and was on the British picket line when the attack was made.

It was from under one of the Bagaduce batteries that Commodore Edward Preble, then a young lieutenant on the Winthrop, later in the war made that brilliant capture of the British brig.

Fort George, at Castine, is now one of the best preserved forts of the Revolutionary period, from the fact that it was restored for use in the war of 1812. There were seven additional batteries erected by the British on Bagaduce Point during the Revolutionary war. It was from Fort George that Gen. Wadsworth made his celebrated and remarkable escape in June, 1781, which is fully recorded in President Dwight's Travels in New England, the facts no doubt coming from the General himself.

Probably the remarkable success of the militia in the Louisburg Expedition, in 1745, had much to do with the assurance of the people in embarking in the hastily formed Bagaduce Expedition, in 1779. Many of the veterans of the siege of Louisburg were then living, and their sons thought themselves no less gallant than their fathers. In fact, the success at Louisburg had much to do with the assurance of the colonists that they could gain their independence from England and no doubt stimulated them, especially in New England, to make the attempt.

The next year after the Bagaduce expedition, Gen. Wadsworth was placed in command of the Department of Maine, and with Col. Joseph Prime's regiment of our state guarded our coast and Penobscot Bay. No further attempt was made to dislodge the British at Castine, and there they remained until December, 1783, when they evacuated the place, as peace had been declared and the war was over.

The following are copies of the original pay-rolls that are now on file in the State House at Boston.

OFFICERS OF THE ARMY.

"A Pay Abstract of the Genl and Staff Officers of the Penobscot Expedition for the Con'l pay, 1779."

	Entered Service.	Wages per Month.
Solomon Lovell, Brig. Genl,	July 2	£37 10sh.
P. Wadsworth, do.	" 8	£37 10 "
Eliphalet Downer, Surg. Genl.,	" 8	£22 10 "
Gowen Brown, Brigade Major,	" 2	£22 4 "
William Todd, do.	" 2	£22 4 "
Jeremiah Hill, Adjt. Genl.	" 2	£15
John Marston, Secy.	" 2	£15
John Tyler, Q. M. Genl.	" 2	£22 10 "
G. W. Speakman, Comy of Ord.,	" 8	£15
Benja. Furness, D. Q. M.,	" 2	£12
J. Robbins, D. C. of Ord.,	" 8	£12
And 3 servants as privates		£2

The originals of the above pay-roll are in the Massachusetts Archives, Vol. XXXVII, Pages 93 and 131.

Col. Jonathan Mitchell's Regiment.

"A Pay Roll for Field and Staff officers in a Regiment of militia Raised in the County of Cumberland, commanded by Jona. Mitchell Esq., in the service of the United States against the enemy at Penobscot in 1779, for Continental Pay."

	Entered service.	Discharged.	Wages.
Jonathan Mitchell, Colo.,	July 1	Sept. 25	£45
Nathaniel Jordan, Lieut. Colo.,	" 6	" 25	£40
Jacob Brown, 1st Major,	" 6	" 25	£35
Nathaniel Larrabee, 2d Major,	" 6	" 25	£35
Thomas Lancaster, Chaplain,	" 6	Aug. 10, at Penobscot,	£40
Nathaniel Jones, Surgeon,	" 6	died, Sept, 4	£40
Benja Porter, Sr., Surgeon's Mate,	" 6	Sept. 4	£30
Gideon Meserve, Adjutant,	" 6	" 25	£30
Enoch Frost, Sergt. Major,	" 6	" 25	£30
Nathaniel Hinkley, Qr. Master,	" 6	" 25	£25

North Yarmouth, Dec. 10, 1779.

Jona. Mitchell, Colo.

The wages are as given on the last roll, evidently a corrected one. The original rolls are in the Massachusetts Archives, Volume XXXVII, pages 103 and 137.

COL. JONATHAN MITCHELL.

Col. Mitchell was from North Yarmouth, and had served in the French and Indian War. He was an ensign in Col. Samuel Waldo, Jr.'s, regiment in 1762, and later a lieutenant. At Falmouth Neck he was prominent in the Revolution, and March 29, 1776, was chosen colonel to succeed Gen. Joseph Frye in command there. He was also colonel of the Second Cumberland County militia regiment, besides commanding this one at Bagaduce.

Jonathan Mitchell was the son of Deacon Jacob and Mary (Howland) Mitchell and was born in 1724. He was a blacksmith, came from Kingston about 1743, and married Sarah Loring. They had several children.

LIEUT. COL. NATHANIEL JORDAN.

Lieut. Col. Jordan was a son of Maj. Dominicus and Joanna (Bray) Jordan, and was born at Spurwink, December 24, 1718; married, August 2, 1740, Hannah Woodbury of Beverly, and had nine children.

He served in the French and Indian War, serving as ensign in Capt. Dominicus Jordan's Snowshoe company in 1744, in the same captain's Training Company in 1757, and was first major and lieutenant colonel of the 1st. Cumberland County militia regiment in 1776, and later, and served in this regiment in 1779, also commanded the militia at Falmouth Neck after the discharge of this regiment.

1ST MAJOR JACOB BROWN.

Major Brown was from North Yarmouth and married, July 13, 1743, Lydia Weare, daughter of Capt. Peter and Sarah (Felt) Weare.

He was a lieutenant in Col. Samuel Waldo, Jr.'s regiment in 1764, enlisted, April 24, 1775, as major in Col. Edmund Phinney's 31st Regiment of Foot, in the 18th Continental regiment in 1776, and in this regiment in 1779.

2D MAJOR NATHANIEL LARRABEE.

Major Larrabee was the son of Capt. Benjamin and Mary (Eilthorpe) Larrabee of Brunswick, and was born in Fort George, December 23, 1729, married, in 1758, Elizabeth Harding, and was town clerk and selectman of his town for many years. He commanded a company on the seacoast at Falmouth in 1775, was a major in the 2d. Cumberland County militia regiment in

1776 and served in this in 1779. The following is a copy of his appointment in Col. Mitchell's regiment.

Major Larrabee : —

Sir : I have orders to rase a Regement out of my Brigade to go to penobscot in order to Dislodge the Enemy there, I do therefore appoint you Second major of Said Regement and expect you will hold yourself In Readyness to march at the shortest notice.

SAMUEL THOMPSON Brigdr.

To Major Nathl. Larrabee.

CHAPLAIN THOMAS LANCASTER.

Chaplain Lancaster was a native of Rowley, Massachusetts, and was the son of Capt. Thomas and Dorothy (Northend) Lancaster, having been born, January 24, 1743. He graduated at Harvard College, in 1764, settled at Scarborough as minister of the First church, November 8, 1775, where he was pastor for fifty-five years. His first marriage was to Lydia Jones, a daughter of Dr. Benjamin and Mary (Woodbury) Jones of Beverly, Massachusetts, and she was a sister to Surgeon Nathaniel Jones of this regiment. His second marriage was to Esther (Libby) Libby, the widow of Mathias. He had Sally, Sewall, Thomas, Jr., Mary, Dorothy, who died when a young lady, and several children who died in infancy. He died, January 12, 1831, aged eighty-seven years.

SURGEON NATHANIEL JONES.

Surgeon Jones went from Cape Elizabeth. He was born February 8, 1743, and was the son of Dr. Benjamin and Mary (Woodbury) Jones of Beverly, Massachusett. He married, in 1766, Sarah Dodge of Ipswich and had seven children. He moved to Cape Elizabeth in 1765, and lived there near the ferry landing, becoming one of the leading patriots of the town. He was a committee of correspondence and delegate to the Cumberland County Congress. He died from exposure in the retreat with his regiment from Bagaduce, September 4, 1779, aged thirty-six years.

SURGEON'S MATE BENJAMIN JONES PORTER.

Surgeon's Mate Porter went from Topsham. He was the son of Capt. "Billy" Porter of the 11th Massachusetts regiment from Beverly, Massachusetts. He married Elizabeth L. King, daughter of Richard King, and practised medicine in Scarborough, Westbrook and Portland. He was "a man of rare conversational powers and great suavity of manners," was a member of the governor's council and senator from Lincoln County. He removed to Camden in 1829 and died August 18, 1847, aged eighty-four years.

ADJ. GIDEON MESERVE.

Adj. Meserve went from Scarborough, and was the son of Deacon Daniel and Mehitable (Bragdon) Meserve. He was born June 31, 1749; married, about 1775, Elizabeth Fogg, and had eleven children.

SERGT. MAJOR ENOCH FROST.

Sergt. Major Frost went from Gorham. He was a retailer there and married, April 24. 1780, Alice Davis, and had Rufus, who died in infancy, Cyrus, Rebecca, Polly, Mason, Coleman, Nathaniel Bowman, Patty and Cyrus for children.

QUARTERMASTER NATHANIEL HINKLEY.

He went from Brunswick, and was, perhaps, son of Samuel and Sarah (Miller) Hinkley.

He served in Capt. Richard Mayberry's Company in Col. Ebenezer Francis' Regiment at Dorchester in 1776 and also in this regiment in 1779.

CAPT. PETER WARREN'S COMPANY.

This company was raised at Falmouth Neck, now Portland.

Capt. Warren came from Somersworth, New Hampshire, and was a cordwainer. He married first, April 16, 1775, Thankful Briggs of Falmouth, and had a daughter who married Capt. Jonathan Tucker. Mrs. Warren died February 27, 1777, aged twenty-five years. He married second, December 30, 1778, Anne Proctor, daughter of Benjamin, and lived on Fore Street between Market and Silver Streets, called now the Market Lot. He had by this marriage seven children, and she died November 9, 1811, aged fifty-six years. He married third, Eunice Libby and moved to Waterford, where he died in 1825, aged seventy-four years. He was a prominent man at Portland and was selectman for four years. He was sergeant in Capt. Joseph Noyes' company at Falmouth six months in 1775, captain of this company in 1779, and also in Capt. Sam'l McCobb's regiment in 1781.

First Lieut. Daniel Mussey was the oldest son of Benjamin and Abigail (Weeks) Mussey. His father was a prominent patriot at Falmouth Neck, in the commencement of the troubles with England. Daniel

Mussey married April 25, 1782, Betsey Baker, who died November 25, 1835, aged seventy-seven years. He died August 31, 1828, aged seventy-three years. Both are buried in the Eastern Cemetery. They lived in a story and a half house on the east corner of Brown and Congress Streets, Portland, and the property is still [1898] owned by his descendants. . Mr. Mussey served as third corporal in Capt. David Bradish's company, in Col. Phinney's 31st regiment of foot in 1775, at Cambridge.

Second Lieut. Peter Babb married, January 24, 1760, Ann Haskell. He was a private in Capt. John Brackett's company in the Lexington alarm, second lieutenant in Capt. Joseph Pride's company in Col. Reuben Fogg's Cumberland County militia regiment, chosen December 9, 1776 ; also in Capt. John Starbird's company in 1st Cumberland County regiment, commissioned February 1, 1777 ; also in this regiment at Bagaduce in 1779.

"A Pay Roll of Capt. Peter Warren's Compy in the Battallion of Malitia Commanded by Jona Mitchell, Esq. on an expedition against Penobscot."

Falmouth, Sept. 25, 1779.

	Date of Enlistment.
Peter Warren, Captain,	July 1, 1779
Daniel Mussey, First Lieut.,	do.
Peter Babb, Second Lieut.,	do.
John Dole, Sergt.,	do.
Stephen Tukey, Sergt.,	do.
Isaac Mirick, Sergt.,	do.
Micah Sampson, Sergt.,	do.
Hugh McLellan, Corp.,	do.
John Clough, Corp.,	do.
Josiah Bayley, Corp.,	do.

Samuel Knight, Corp.,	July 1, 1799	
William Moody, Drummer,	do.	
William Harper, Fifer,	do.	

PRIVATES.

Benjamin Mussey,	July 1, 1779.	
Daniel Cobb,	do.	
David Warren,	do.	
Daniel Green,	do.	
Ebenr Owen,	do.	
Elijah Ward,	do.	
Ebenr Gustin,	do.	
Eleazer Whitney,	do.	Not joined after the retreat.
Houchin Tukey,	do.	
Isaac Randall,	do.	
Isaac Larrabee,	do.	Not joined after the retreat.
John Fogg,	do.	do.
Joseph Morse,	do.	
John Hans,	do.	
John Masury,	do.	
Jonathan Sawyer,	do.	
James Hans,	do.	
John D. Smith,	do.	
Joseph Stanford,	do.	
Josiah Shaw,	do.	
Joseph Thomas,	do.	
Jeremiah Brackett,	do.	
John Small,	do.	
Josiah Walker,	do.	
John Roe,	do.	
James Rand,	do.	
Joseph Johnson,	do.	
Henry Waite,	do.	
Lemuel Cox,	do.	
Moses Brazier,	do.	
Nathl Moody,	do.	
Nathl Libby,	do.	
Peter Kelley,	do.	
Paul Dyer,	do.	Not joined after the retreat.
Richard Codman,	do.	
Richard Fassett,	do.	
Robert Poage,	do.	
Somers Shattuck,	do.	

Samuel Larrabee,	July 1, 1799	Not joined after the retreat.
Thomas Gustin,	do.	do.
Woodbury Storer,	do.	(Appointed clerk to the Adjt. Gen.) Aug. 1.
Wheeler Riggs,	do.	Killed ye 7th August, 1779.
William Maxwell,	do.	
Zach Baker,	do.	

Total, 57 men

The wages and terms of service were as follows:

Captain,	$40.00 per month,	2 mos.,	25 days service.
First Lieut.,	$26⅔ " "	2 "	25 " "
Second Lieut.,	$26⅔ " "	2 "	25 " "
Sergeants,	$10.00 " "	2 "	18 " "
Corporals and Musicians	$7½ " "	2 "	18 " "
Privates,	$6⅔ " "	2 "	18 " "

Cumberland, Ss., Dec. 3, 1779, Captain Peter Warren and Daniel Mussey made oath to the Truth of the foregoing Pay Roll for their Company in the Expedition against Penobscot under the command of Jonathan Mitchell, Esq., and that the several Persons borne on Said Roll served the Time thereon mentioned.

CORAM ENOCH FREEMAN, *Justo Pacis.*

The original of this roll is in the Massachusetts Archives, Vol. XXXVII, Page 102.

CAPT. JOSHUA JORDAN'S COMPANY.

This company went from the town of Cape Elizabeth.

Capt. Joshua Jordan was the son of Nathaniel and Dorothy Jordan, and was born at Spurwink, in 1736. He married March 24, 1763, Catherine Jordan, a daughter of Richard and Katherine (Hanscom) Jordan. They had eight children, and he died at Richmond Island. Capt. Jordan was a training soldier in Capt. Dominicus Jordan's company, in 1757, captain in Col. Peter Noyes' militia regiment, November 20, 1778, and served in this regiment.

First Lieut. Dominicus Mitchell had a wife, Anne, and they acknowledged the covenant in the First Parish church, Falmouth, September 7, 1766. He served as lieutenant in Samuel Whitmore's company, in Col. Reuben Fogg's regiment, and is said to have gone to Peekskill, New York.

Second Lieut. Lemuel Dyer married Sarah Jones, in 1782. He was licensed a retailer in 1783, and may have had other service than that in this regiment.

"A Pay Role For the commissioned and non-commissioned officers and soldiers in Capt. Joshua Jordan's Company in Col. Jonathan Mitchell's Regt. in an Expedition against Penobscot From the 7th of July to the 25th of Sept. 1779— in the Continental service."

Joshua Jordan,	Capt.
Dominicus Mitchell,	1st. Lieut.
Lemuel Dyer,	2d Lieut.
Tristum Jordan,	Sergt.
Peter Sanborn,	"
John Thorndick,	Sergt.
Soloman Jordan,	"
Abner Fickett,	Corp.
Josiah Black,	"
Dan'l Roberson,	"
Ebenezer Sawyer,	"
Abraham Jordan,	Drummer.
Robert Thorndike,	Fifer.

PRIVATES.

Moses Hanson
Zachariah Leach
Lemuel Dyer, Jr.
Thomas Jordan
Joseph Maxwell
Samuel Jordan
James Jordan
John Maxwell
William Maxwell
James Miller

Thos. Cummins
Ebenezer Shaw
John Hall
David Sanborn
Benjamin Swett
Joseph Chace
Jacob York
Robert Row
Saml Batchlor
Richard Pierce

Zebulon Ficket
David Parker
George Strout
Nath'l Cash
Richard Wescott
Enoch Strout
Samuel Crockett
Elkeny Dyer
John Orion
Eli Jaxson

John Strout
Wm. Freeman
Mark Dyer
Jacob Sawyer
Ezekiel Sawyer
James Mitchell
Patrick Irish
John Fickett
Batholemo Jaxson
Isaac Dyer

Total, 53 men.

The original pay-rolls of this company are in the Massachusetts Archives, Volume **XXXVII**, pages 85 and 126.

CAPT. NEHEMIAH CURTIS' COMPANY.

This company was raised in the town of Harpswell.

Capt. Nehemiah Curtis was the son of David and Bethia Curtis, and was born in Hanover, Massachusetts, in 1733. He was a prominent man at Harpswell, and served the town as selectman several years, and during the Revolutionary War was a committee of safety. He lived near Center Harpswell. His death occurred December 26, 1816, at the age of eighty-three years. In the old graveyard, near where he lived, he was buried, and from his gravestone I copied this epitaph.

A true Patriot, commanded the Militia before and during the revolutionary war, discharged with honor & fidelity the several offices he held & hath left an imitable pattern.

First Lieut. Isaac Hall was probably the son of Isaac and Abigail Hall of Harpswell. His wife's name was Joanna and he was probably the ferryman at Sebascodegan Island.

Second Lieut. Ebenezer Stanwood belonged in Brunswick and was a licensed innholder, 1771-1785, and a retailer in 1793.

"A Pay Roll for Capt. Nehemiah Curtis' Company in Col. Jonathan Mitchell's Regt in the Service of the United States in the Expedition at Penobscot from the 7th day of July to the 25th day of September inclusive, 1779."

Nehemiah Curtis,	Capt.
Isaac Hall,	1st Lieut.
Eben'r Stanwood,	2nd "
Marlboro Sylvester,	Serg't.
Elnathan Hinkley,	"
Kingsbury Eastman,	"
Wm. Dunning,	"
David Given,	Corp.
Wm. Tarr,	"
John Spear,	"
Caleb Curtis,	"
Ezekiel Brown,	Drummer.
Daniel Webber,	Fifer.

PRIVATES.

Samuel Stanwood	Wm. Getchell
Robert Stanwood	Stephen Rideout
Isaac Chase	Fields Coombs
Josiah Clark	Wm. Curtis
Daniel Booker	Hezekiah Coombs
Wm. Mallet	Phinehas Thomson
John Blake	Asa Coombs
James Barstow	John Jordan
Isaiah Booker	James Chase
Nehemiah Ward	Benj. Getchel
Wm. Wilson	Robert Purington
Joseph Ewing	Hudson Bishop
Wm. McLellan	John Linscot
James Ross	Benj. Sleeper
David Doughty	Joseph Woodward
Nathl Ham	David Dunning
John Andross	John Dunning
Calvin Cowen	Abraham Rideout

Thos. Morgareidge	Jedediah Allen
Swanzy Wilson	Wm. Woodside
Nehemiah Ward, Jr.	Wm. Starboard
Joseph Webber	Hugh Dunlap
John Ferrin	Silas Kemp
Joseph Tompson	James Bibber
Lemuel Rament	David Johnson
Mathew Martin	Joseph Ross
Joseph Webber	John Larrabee
Peter Williams	Saml Hunt
John Crawford	Asa Millar
Thos. Ham	Abner Purington

Total, 73 men.

Josiah Clark, Wm. Mallet, Isaiah Booker and David Johnson were allowed two months and eight days' service, Joseph Ross, two months and fifteen days, and all others, two months and eighteen days. The men were allowed seventy-six miles travel in marching home. Three of this company deserted, August 4, and the History of Harpswell says some of the men never received any pay. There are two original pay-rolls in the Massachusetts Archives, one in Volume XXXV, page 251, and another in Volume XL, page 120.

CAPT. NATHAN MERRILL'S COMPANY.

This company was raised from the towns of New Gloucester, Windham, Gray, Poland and Turner. They were credited with two months and seventeen days service.

Capt. Nathan Merrill belonged in Gray and, in 1776, served as first lieutenant in Capt. Winthrop Baston's company at the seige of Boston, in Col. Jacob French's regiment. He was also a captain in Col. Mitchell's regiment in 1779, and took a British corporal prisoner at Bagaduce, July 31. He probably went from Falmouth to Gray, and from there to New Gloucester.

First Lieut. Edward Anderson went from Windham. He was the son of Abraham Anderson and was born May 10, 1753, married August 4, 1774, Mary Mayberry, a daughter of Capt. Richard and Martha (Bolton) Mayberry; she was born November 10, 1756, and died May 20, 1846. aged eighty-nine years. They had eleven sons and one daughter, and he died May 17, 1804, aged fifty-one years.

Lieut. Anderson settled at the foot of Windham Hill, where he built a house and saw mill. He was the first postmaster of the town, selectman and was a colonel in the militia. His service in the army was as lieutenant in Capt. Samuel Knight's company, July 1, 1775, and served at Falmouth six months and sixteen days, also was second lieutenant in Capt. Thomas Trott's company of 4th Cumberland County militia commissioned in September, 1777, besides his service in Col. Mitchell's regiment at Bagaduce in 1779.

Second Lieut. Peter Graffam was a son of Caleb and Lois (Bennett) Graffam, of Windham, and was born at Falmouth, April 3, 1742. He married, February 16, 1764, Mary Wilson, and settled in New Gloucester before 1770, where he had a sawmill. He was a housewright and died about 1784. We know of no other service in this army than that in Col. Mitchell's regiment in 1779.

" Muster Roll of Capt. Nathan Merrill's Company of Militia Raised in the County of Cumberland for the expedition against the Penobscot,

For the Service of the United States and served in a Detachment Commanded by Col. Jonathan Mitchell."

Marched July 8, and were discharged Sept. 25, 1779.

Nathan Merrill,	Capt.
Edward Anderson,	1st Lieut.
Peter Graffum,	2d Lieut.
John Elder,	Sergt.
Richard Haden,	"
Thos. Mabury,	"
John Marshall,	"
Asa Libby,	Corp.
John Hodge,	"
Joseph Elder,	"
Francis Bennit,	"
Isaac Cummings,	Drummer
John McGuyer,	Fifer

PRIVATES.

James Mabury,
Benj. Trott,
Thomas Chute,
Nathl Chase,
John Mugford,
Samuel Lord,
Samuel Toben,
George Knight,
Joseph Roberts,
Nemiah Allen,
Samuel Todd,
Samuel Bradbury,
James Allan,
Stephen Row.
John Harris,
Benj. Witham,
David Paul.
Joshua Clark,
Joseph Collins,
James Stevens,
Samuel Tarbox,
John Chandler,

Saml Nevens,
Edward Ryou.
James Noyes,
Isaac Eoly,
Thomas Millett,
Zeptha Benson,
Joshua Strout.
Aaron Davis,
Job Denning,
Saml Morgan,
Wm. Cordwell,
Jona Saunders,
Wm. Libby,
Job Young,
Amos Hobbs,
Nathan Noble, Jr.
Daniel Knight,
Benj. Jones,
Mark Andros,
Moses Merrill,
Abner Phillips,
Joshua Lain,
Nathl Stevens.

Total, 58 men.

The original pay-roll is in the Massachusetts Archives, Vol. XXXVII, Page 120.

CAPT. BENJAMIN LARRABEE'S COMPANY.

This company was raised in the town of Scarborough.

Capt. Benjamin Larrabee was the son of Benjamin and Sarah Larrabee of Scarborough, and was born March 23, 1740. He married, June 28, 1778, Hannah (Hasty) Skillings, the widow of Capt. John Skillings of the 11th Massachusetts regiment, and died April 17, 1829, aged eighty-nine years. Capt. Larrabee commanded a company at Falmouth Neck in October and November 1775, served in Col. Reuben Fogg's militia regiment, and in 1779 in Col. Mitchell's regiment. After the war, he was a colonel in the militia and a representative to the General Court.

First Lieut. Josiah Libby was the son of Josiah and Anna (Small) Libby of Scarborough, and was born February 16, 1746. He married first, in 1769, Eunice Libby; second, in 1776, Elizabeth (Parcher) Foss; and third, Mary (Chase) Jones. He died March 1, 1824, aged seventy-eight years. Lieut. Libby served in Capt. John Wentworth's company, Col. Aaron Willard's regiment in 1776 and in Col. Mitchell's regiment in 1779.

Second Lieut. Lemuel Milliken was the son of Edward and Abigail (Norman) Milliken, of Scarborough, and married January 18, 1770, Phebe Lord. They had at least seven children, Abraham, Mary, Susan, Margaret, Samuel, Phebe and Jacob.

Lieut. Milliken served as a sergeant in Capt. John Rice's company in Col. Phinney's 31st regiment of foot in 1775, and Col. Mitchell's regiment in 1779.

"A Pay Roll of Benjamin Larrabee's Company belonging to Col. Mitchell's Regiment in ye Expedition against Penobscot."

"All marched July 9th. Discharged Sept. 12th."

Benjamin Larrabee,	Capt.
Josiah Libby,	1st Lieut,
Lemuel Milliken,	2nd Lieut.
Robert Hasty,	Sergt
Seth Libby,	"
Isaac Davis,	"
Nathl Milliken,	"
Joseph Hodsdon,	Corp.
Humphrey Hanscom,	"
William McLellan,	"
William Shule,	"
John Martin,	Drummer
Jeremiah Banks,	Fifer

PRIVATES.

Daniel Stone,	Robert Edgscom,
Chas Runnels,	Ebenr Sevey,
Martin Jose,	John Andrews,
Thos McKenney,	George Newbegin,
John McKenney,	Thos. Berry,
Mark Libby,	Simeon Beal,
William Mars,	Samuel Libby,
Joseph Brown,	Eleazer Briant,
John Bragdon,	Joel Harmon,
Wm Gilford,	Elias Harmon,
Samuel Plummer,	Nathl Rice,
Joseph Ring,	John Meserve,
Joshua Hutchins,	George Moses,
Soloman Larrabee,	Lemuel Jordan,
Moses Libby,	Jona. Harmon,
William Mitchell,	Joseph Waterhouse,
Gibeon Plummer,	Increse Graffum,
James McKenney,	David Burnam,
Nathan Larrabee,	Levi Morrill,
Simeon Fitz,	Nathan Kimball,
Wm Fenderson,	Ezekiel Foster,
Roberd McKenney,	Abnor Lunt,
Ebenr. Boothby,	John Watson,
Thos. Thurston,	Daul Libby,
Thos. Tompson,	Joseph Tyler,

John Molton,   David Hasty,
Samuel Holms,   Nathan Moses.
  Total, 64 men.

The men of this company were allowed two months and three days service. The original pay-roll is in the Massachusetts Archives, Vol. XXXVII, Page 89.

CAPT. WILLIAM COBB'S COMPANY.

This company was raised in Old Falmouth, on the Presumpscot River. On the retreat they arrived at Camden, August 18.

Capt. William Cobb was the son of Samuel Cobb a shipbuilder, and prominent in the affairs of Old Falmouth in his time. He married, March 2, 1778, Eunice Quimby, a daughter of Joseph and Mary Quimby. He became a colonel in the militia and built the large brick house in Market Square in Portland, which was altered into the American House and burned in 1852. Capt. Cobb served as first lieutenant in Capt. Jesse Partridge's company in Col. John Greaton's 3d Massachusetts regiment, eight months in the army on the Hudson River in 1778, and as captain in Col. Mitchell's regiment at Bagaduce in 1779.

First Lieut. Moses Merrill belonged in Old Falmouth and married, in 1777, Jane Hutchinson. He was a private in Capt. Samuel Noyes' company in Col. Phinney's regiment, in 1775, and first lieutenant in Col. Mitchell's regiment in 1779. He was alive in 1835, aged ninety years.

Second Lieut. Joshua Stevens married February 5, 1767, Susannah Sawyer. He was a sergeant in Capt. John Brackett's company in Col. Phinney's 31st regiment of foot in 1775, and second lieutenant in this company in Col. Mitchell's regiment in 1779.

Ensign Nathaniel Tompson lived in Falmouth. He was the son of Joseph Tompson and had brothers, Edward and Joseph.

Muster Roll of Capt. William Cobb's Company of Militia Raised in the County of Cumberland for an expedition against Penobscot. For the service of the United States and Served in a Detachment commanded by Col Jona Mitchell."

All marched July 8, and were discharged Sept. 25, 1779.

William Cobb,	Capt.
Moses Merrill,	1st. Lieut.
Joshua Stevens,	2nd "
Nath'l Tompson,	Ensign.
Amos Noyes,	Sergt.
Amos Merrill,	"
Moses Noyes,	"
Wm. Brackett,	"
James Merrill,	Corp.
Josiah Lock,	"
Peter Cobb,	"
Benj. McIntire,	"
Josiah Berrey,	Drummer.
Joshua Whitney,	Fifer.

PRIVATES.

Nath'l Wormwell	Ephrm. Lunt
Joseph Wormwell	Zachr. Merrill
Josiah Clark	James Noyes
Joseph Davis	Josiah Noyes
Jona Knight	Nathan Lunt
Benja Moody	Moses Adams
Amos Knight	Robert Morrison
Moses Blanchard	John Proctor
Tobias Goold	Joseph Pride
Thos. Merrill	Isaac Sawyer
Israel Merrill	John Sawyer
James Merrill, Jr.	Charles Walker
Jona Sawyer	Stephen Knight
Nathl Tripp	Joseph Merrill

John Thurlo	Mark Knight
Nathl Patrick	Thos. Knight
Jos. Stapels	Joshua Dunn
James Roberts	Jona Sawyer
Stephen Dodd	Amos Knight
Wm. Titcomb	John Merrill
Benj. Pettengell	Nathl Noyes
David Underwood	Joshua Brackett
Wm. Dodd	Nathl Gordon
John Brackett	Saml. Swett
Thos. Doughty	Peter Hammond
Edmund Merrill	Page Tobey
Edmund Merrill, Jr.	John Brown
James Frank	John Plummer

Total, 70 men.

There are two original pay-rolls of this company in the Massachusetts Archives, Volume XXXVII, pages 117 and 135.

CAPT. ALEXANDER McLELLAN'S COMPANY.

This company was raised in Gorham, and it is said they suffered severely in their retreat of eighty or ninety miles through the wild and uncultivated country and that several perished on the way.

Capt. Alexander McLellan was the son of Hugh and Elizabeth McLellan of Gorham, and was born about 1741. He married, October 21, 1765, Margaret Johnson, a daughter of James and Jane Johnson, of Stroudwater; she was born in 1739. Their children were Jenny, died young; James, died young; Isaac, William, Nelly, Alexander, James and Jenny. Capt. McLellan, from overexertion, anxiety, and exposure in the retreat from Bagaduce, was seized with a fever and died October 4, 1779, aged about thirty-eight years. His widow married for her second husband,

L. of C.

April 15, 1781, John Miller of Gorham. Rev. Elijah Kellogg, a grandson of Capt. McLellan's sister Mary, wrote that he was one "who was a very devil for grit."

First Lieut. Ebenezer Murch of Gorham, married in 1763, Margaret Phillips of Pepperrellboro, now Saco, and had Joseph, Jeremiah, Isaac, John, Lydia, Moses, Aaron, Sally, Betty and Ebenezer, Jr.

Second Lieut. Joseph Knight lived in Gorham near South Windham, where he purchased land in 1767. He erected a sawmill and carried on the lumbering business. He married January 10, 1760, Lydia Libby, a daughter of John and Mary (Miller) Libby of Scarboro, who was born June 5, 1743. He was drowned while working about his mill September 9, 1797, aged sixty-two years. They had Lydia, Phebe, Nathaniel, Daniel, Joseph, Nabby, Joseph, Samuel, Morris, Winthrop and Benjamin.

"A Pay Roll for Capt. Alexander McLellan's Company in Col. Jonathan Mitchell's Regt. in the Expedition against the Enemy at Penobscot it being for the pay from the Massachusetts State—1779."

All entered service July 7 and were discharged Sept. 25, 1779.

Alexander McLellan,	Capt.
Ebenezer Murch,	1st Lieut.
Joseph Knight,	2nd Lieut.
Thomas Irish,	Sergt.
George Strout,	"
Stephen Whitney,	"
John Emory,	"
Daniel Whitney,	Corp.
Jeremiah Hodsdon,	"
Samuel File,	"
Joseph McDonald,	"
John Lakeman,	Drummer.

PRIVATES.

Edmund Phinney, Jr.	Charles McDonald
Benjamin Haskell	Joseph Irish

Moses Hauscom	William Meserve
John Blanchard	Uriel Whitney
John Gammau	Joseph Jones
Joseph Gamman	Seth Harding
Samuel Murch	Gershon Davis
John Phinney	Daniel Whitmore
Nathl. Bacon	Abner Jordan
Wm. McLellan	Moses Jordan
Lazarus Rand	John Elwell
James Murch	William Irish
Richard Lombard	James Stubbs
Prince Hamblen	John Davis
John Parker	Samuel Rounds
Josiah Swett	William File
Peter White	Joshua Davis
Daniel Whitney	William Wood
Joseph Brackett	Abel Whitney
John Meserve	Stephen Powell
Wm. Murch	Asa Thurlo
Edward Wilson	John Hermon
Zachariah Weston	James Huntress
John Akers	Samuel Whitney
Benjamin Stevens	Isaac Chase
Ebenezer Whitney	James Watson
Reujamin Roberts	Stephen Sawyer

John Smith

Total, 67 men,

The wages in this pay-roll are given as follows : —

Captain,	£30	per month
Lieutenants,	£24	" "
Sergeants,	£23	" "
Corporals,	£22	" "
Privates,	£21	" "

The original pay-roll is in the Massachusetts Archives, Volume XXXVII, page 83, and there is another on page 128.

Capt. John Gray's Company.

This company was raised at North Yarmouth.

Capt. John Gray was the son of Andrew and Phebe (Chandler) Gray and was born November 29, 1732.

He married in November, 1755, Sarah Mitchell, a daughter of Deacon Jacob and Rachel (Lewis) (Cushing) Mitchell, who died May 27, 1796, aged sixty years. He died December 27, 1796, aged sixty-four years. They had five boys and seven girls. He was a shipmaster and farmer and lived at North Yarmouth.

First Lieut. John Soule was the son of Barnabas and Jane (Bradbury) Soule and was born March 12, 1740. He married first, November 30, 1763, Elizabeth Mitchell, a daughter of Benjamin and Mehitable (Bragdon) Mitchell. She was born September 29, 1747, and died December 26, 1794. He married second, October 10, 1795, Elizabeth Stanwood of Brunswick, who died April 26, 1800, and he married third, April 17, 1814, Chloe Josselyn, who died September 26, 1831. His children were Mehitable, Dorcas, Cornelius, Benjamin, John. Elizabeth, Bradbury, Joanna, Rufus, Joseph and Barnabas. He was a sea captain.

Lieut. Soule was a lieutenant in the militia at North Yarmouth in 1776, also in Col. Mitchell's regiment in 1779, in the Bagaduce Expedition.

Second Lieut. Ozias Blanchard was the son of Nathaniel and Hannah (Shaw) Blanchard, and was born in Weymouth, Massachusetts, July 31, 1742. He married in 1769, Mercy Soule, the daughter of Barnabas and Jane (Bradbury) Soule, and, therefore, a sister to Lieut. John Soule of this company. She was born November 27, 1749. They had Samuel, Jeremiah, David, Reuben, Daniel and Olive.

Lieut. Blanchard was a sergeant in Captain George Roger's company of the 2d Cumberland County militia regiment, and served six days fortifying Falmouth Neck in November, 1775. He was second lieutenant in Capt. John Worthley's company in Col. Reuben Fogg's militia regiment, December 9, 1776, also commissioned January 14, 1777, in Capt. John Gray's company in the militia, and served in Col. Mitchell's regiment in 1779, two months and six days at Bagaduce. He was a lieutenant colonel in the militia in 1792.

"A Pay Roll for Capt. John Gray's Company in Col. Jonathan Mitchell's Regt. of Militia in the Service of the United States in the Expedition at Penobscot from the 7th of July to the 12th of Sept. inclusive, 1779."

		Wages.
John Gray,	Capt.	£12
John Soule,	1st. Lieut.	£8, 2 sh.
Ozias Blanchard,	2nd. "	£8, 2 "
Joseph Ludden,	Sergt.	£2, 8 "
James Pittee,	"	£2, 8 "
Robt. Anderson,	"	£2, 8 "
James Rogers,	"	£2, 8 "
Ezekiel Loring,	Q. M. Sergt.	discharged, Aug. 23. £2, 4 sh.
Samuel Talbot,	Corp.	died Sept. 25.
James Crocker,	"	£2, 4 sh.
Calvin Carver,	"	£2, 4 "
John Winslow,	"	£2, 4 "
Jacob Brown, Jr.,	Drummer.	£2, 4 "
Davis Woodward, Jr.,	Fifer.	£2, 4 "

PRIVATES.

Joe Sweetser	Josh Lake
Seth Blanchard	Joseph Brewer
Richard Stubbs, Jr.	Jas. Anderson, Jr.
Jonathan True	Edward Parker
John Davis	Geo. Bartol
Benj. Winslow	Danl. Carter
Saml. Lawrence	Burrel Tuttle
Amos Harris, Jr.	Nath. Weeks
Wm. Buxton	Abner Dennison, Jr.
James Pomroy	Tho. Sylvester
Wm. Ring	Moses Roberts, discharged Aug 25

Wm. Bradbury	Levi Marston
Josiah Wyman	Josiah Reed
Barna Soul	Nathan Aldridge
Joseph Humphrey	Jacob Merrill
Danl. Worthley	Tho. Burrows
John Oakes	John Drinkwater, Jr.
Ephm. Brown	Edmond Titcomb, Jr.
Isaac Royal, discharged Aug. 23.	Wm. Soul
Amaziah Delano	Benaiah Fogg
Nathl. Mitchell, discharged Aug. 23.	Zebulon Tuttle
Danl. Mitchell, Jr.	Josiah Dill
Peter Weare	John Lee
Comfort Videto	Wm. True
Thos. Pearson, Jr.	Joseph Davis, discharged Aug. 23
Soloman Williams	Ezekiel Hacket, " " "
Total, 66 men.	

The privates' wages were £2 per month, and the
original pay-roll of this company is in the Massachusetts Archives, Volume XXXVI, page 18.

The people of America are appreciating more and
more, each year, the value of the services of the suffering soldiers of the Revolution. Their victories
were few and their defeats many, but their resolute
devotion to a cause which they believed just, and time
has proved it so, commands the admiration and respect
of all lovers of liberty. The regiments that suffered
in defeat and disaster were a part of the noble army
of men that gained for us our independence, and will
always be honored for what they attempted to do
towards that end.

"The contest was long, bloody and affecting.
Righteous heaven approved the solemn appeal, victory
crowned their arms, and the peace, liberty and independence of the United States of America was their
glorious reward."

www.ingramcontent.com/pod-product-compliance
Lightning Source LLC
Chambersburg PA
CBHW030027030726
47499CB00008B/3152